English Country

A TASTE (

ESSEⱯ

The Yeoman Country

A Selection of Traditional Local Recipes

AN ESSEX PASTORAL

Compiled by
Michelle Carter

With paintings by L. Burleigh Bruhl R.B.A.
and drawings by Frederick L. Griggs R.A.

SALMON

AUDLEY END NEAR SAFFRON WALDEN

Published by J Salmon Limited,
100 London Road, Sevenoaks, Kent TN13 1BB

Designed by the Salmon Studio
Copyright © 1995 J Salmon Limited
ISBN 1 898435 39 1

Printed in England by J Salmon Limited, Tubs Hill Works, Sevenoaks, Kent

Front Cover Picture: Thaxted from the Elsenham Road
Back Cover Picture: Passingford Mill on the Roding

Index

HIGH RODING

ST. JOHN'S ABBEY GATE, COLCHESTER

Essex Pudding Pies

A rice and custard dish baked as individual puddings.

1½ oz. ground rice	3 eggs
¾ pint milk	Pinch of salt
1½ oz. butter	Grated nutmeg
2 oz. sugar	3 oz. currants
8 oz. shortcrust pastry	

Set oven to 400°F or Mark 6. In a saucepan, boil the ground rice in the milk for 15 minutes. Remove from the heat and stir in the butter and the sugar. Beat the eggs well and add them to the rice mixture together with the salt and nutmeg. Beat well and leave to cool, but not set. Roll out the pastry on a lightly floured surface and use it to line 8 small, greased 6 oz. pudding basins. Fill each basin ¾-full with the rice mixture and sprinkle with currants on top. Bake for 15 minutes. Serves about 6.

Smoked Oyster Parcels

Colchester is the centre of Essex oyster growing and the ancient Colchester Oyster Feast is held in October. Oysters and Colchester, the Camulodunum of the Romans, have been linked since early Roman times.

3 x 4 oz. cans smoked oysters	1 teaspoon fresh or dried
3 hardboiled eggs, peeled	dill, chopped
and finely chopped	Salt and pepper
5 oz. fresh brown bread-	12 medium sized spinach
crumbs	leaves

Cut the oysters in half and place in a bowl with their juice. Add the finely chopped hard-boiled eggs, breadcrumbs and dill and blend together. Season. Wash the spinach leaves and remove most of the stems. Steam them for exactly one minute and cool under cold running water. Pat dry each leaf with kitchen paper. Place two teaspoons of the stuffing mixture on to the stem end of a spinach leaf, roll over once, then fold in the sides and roll again to the end so that you have a small, enclosed sausage. Repeat with all the leaves. Then steam the parcels for 10 minutes and serve hot as a starter. Serves 4.

Maldon Boiled Beef

A warming meal made with the famous Maldon Sea Salt.

1 piece of topside or	Bunch of herbs
silverside of beef	2 cloves
1 carrot	Peppercorns
1 onion, peeled	Water
1 leek	Maldon Crystal Salt

Peel the onion and stud with the cloves. Scrub the carrot, wash the leek and place with the meat and all the other ingredients, except the salt, in a saucepan. Cover with water, bring to the boil and simmer until the meat is cooked and tender. Lift the meat out of the stock on to a serving dish. Serve the meat sliced, with a good grinding of Maldon Crystal Sea Salt over each slice, together with accompanying vegetables. The stock can be used for soup. Serves 4.

Essex Scrap-cakes

These cakes are very wholesome for children and the resulting home-made lard is of generally better quality than the mass-produced product.

1½–2lb. flead (producing	1 oz. candied lemon peel
approx. 6 oz. "scraps")	6 oz. currants
1 lb. plain flour	Milk to mix
4 oz. light soft brown sugar	¼ teaspoon bicarbonate
1 teaspoon ground allspice	of soda

To make the "scraps" take the flead (the fat from the inside of a pig) remove the skin membrane and cut it into small pieces. Place in an ovenproof dish in a hot oven until the fat is reduced to oil, leaving small pieces, or "scraps" floating on the surface. Take care not to let it get too hot; the "scraps" should be crispy but not browned. Strain off the molten lard and set aside to solidify for future use. Set oven to 425°F or Mark 7. In a bowl, rub the cold scraps into the flour and add the sugar, spice, peel and currants. Mix the bicarbonate of soda with the milk and beat well into the mixture to make a thick paste. Spoon into greased small Yorkshire Pudding tins (or similar). Bake for 15–20 minutes until golden brown. Makes about 25–30 cakes.

BEELEIGH ABBEY NEAR MALDON

Onion Pudding

A soft, dough pudding with onions and herbs that is excellent on its own or as an accompaniment to boiled meat.

½ lb. self raising flour	1 dessertspoon mixed herbs
4 oz. shredded suet	1 lb. onions, peeled and chopped
Salt and pepper	Milk and water to mix

In a bowl, mix together the dry ingredients and form a soft dough with the milk and water. Mix in the onions. Put the mixture into a greased pudding basin, cover with greased paper and a cloth or kitchen foil and steam for 2–2½ hours. This pudding is delicious eaten hot with boiled ham or boiled beef. Serves 4–6.

Ugley Duckling

Roast duck with a delicious herb stuffing from the village of Ugley near Saffron Walden.

1 large duck, about 6 lb.	1 teaspoon mixed herbs
Juice of 1 orange	Grated zest of orange
2 oz. shredded suet	Salt and pepper
4 oz. soft breadcrumbs	Duck liver, chopped
Pinch grated nutmeg	Two rashers of streaky
3 teaspoons chopped	bacon, chopped
parsley	1 egg

Orange segments and rashers of streaky bacon for garnish

Set oven to 425°F or Mark 7. Prick the duck breast with a skewer, brush over with the orange juice and sprinkle with salt. Make the stuffing by mixing the breadcrumbs with the suet, add the nutmeg, parsley, mixed herbs and orange zest. Then add the chopped duck liver and chopped bacon rashers. Season. Beat the egg and mix it with the stuffing mixture to bind it. Stuff the duck and place on the highest shelf of the oven for half and hour. Now reduce the oven heat to 350°F, or Mark 4 and roast for a further 2 hours. Transfer to a serving dish, garnish with the segments of orange that have been wrapped in the streaky bacon rashers and then fried. Serves 4.

Tipsy D'Arcy Spice Apples

The D'Arcy Spice apple was first found in the garden of the Hall at Tolleshunt D'Arcy in 1880; they are a late russet variety which is picked in November and keeps until May. If D'Arcy Spice apples are not available, then Egremont Russet will make a satisfactory alternative.

2 lb. D'Arcy spice apples	3 oz. unsalted butter
4 oz. soft brown sugar	1 large glass sweet white wine

Set oven to 450°F or Mark 8. Butter an 11 inch oval, ovenproof dish. Core and slice, but do not peel, the apples. Lay the apple slices in the dish with the slices overlapping. Sprinkle on the sugar and dot with small pieces of the butter. Pour the wine over the top and bake until tender. Serve with single cream. Serves 6.

Essex Hotpot

A quickly made pork hotpot covered with potato and cheese.

1½ lb. lean pork, cubed
2 medium onions, peeled and
  sliced
1 can condensed chicken soup

1 small can peeled tomatoes
6 medium potatoes, peeled
  and sliced
3 oz. Cheddar cheese, grated

Oil for frying

Set oven to 350°F or Mark 4. Remove any bones from the meat and cut into chunky cubes. Fry the onion in a little oil until soft, mix in the meat cubes and brown them quickly on all sides. Transfer to an oven-proof casserole. Add the soup and tomatoes and season to taste. Cover with the sliced potatoes and sprinkle the grated cheese over the top. Cover with foil and cook in the oven for 2–2½ hours. Remove the foil for the last 20 minutes. Serve with a green vegetable. Serves 6.

TOLLESHUNT MAJOR

Debden Tomato and Apple Chutney

A tangy, Bramley apple chutney from the village of Debden midway between Saffron Walden and picturesque Thaxted with its ancient Guildhall.

2 lb. Bramley apples	1 pint vinegar
1 lb. red tomatoes	½ lb. raisins
½ lb. moist brown sugar	1 teaspoon salt
2 oz. onion, chopped	Pinch of cayenne pepper

Peel, slice and core the apples. In a saucepan, cook together the sliced apples, tomatoes, onions, and raisins in the vinegar until soft. Add the sugar, salt and pepper and cook for about a further 20 minutes. The mixture is sufficiently reduced when a channel formed by a wooden spoon drawn through the mixture no longer fills with vinegar. Pot into hot, sterilised jars and seal with plastic lids or jampot covers. Store for at least one month before eating.

Essex Meat Layer Pudding

A filling and warming winter luncheon dish.

SUET PASTRY

6 oz. flour	3 oz. shredded suet
¼ teaspoon salt	½ cup cold water

FILLING

1 tablespoon butter	1 tablespoon chopped chives
2 medium sized onions, sliced	¼ teaspoon black pepper
	½ teaspoon salt
½ lb. minced pork	¼ teaspoon celery salt
½ lb. minced veal or chicken	1 tablespoon plain flour
1 teaspoon dried sage	2 egg yolks
¼ teaspoon dried oregano	2 tablespoons double cream

Pastry: sift the flour and salt into bowl and mix in the suet. Add enough water to make a stiff dough. Wrap in greaseproof paper and put in refrigerator for 10 minutes. Meanwhile make the filling. Fry the onions in the butter until soft and golden. Add the meats, herbs, seasonings and flour, Mix well, cook for 5 minutes and then remove pan from heat. Beat together the egg yolks and cream and add to the meat mixture. Cook for 5 minutes more. Butter a 2½ pint pudding basin. Roll out the dough on a lightly floured to ¼-inch thick. Cut a small circle to fit the bottom of the basin and put in place. Spoon on a layer of meat mixture (about 1½-inches deep) then add another circle of dough to fit and another layer of meat. Continue until the filling and dough have been used up, finishing with a layer of dough, You should have 3 layers of meat mixture. The ingredients will not fill the basin, but there needs to be room for the dough to expand. Cover the basin with greaseproof paper and kitchen foil and steam for 4 hours. Turn out the pudding on to a plate and serve with vegetables. Serves 4.

BEAUMONT HALL, BEAUMONT-CUM-MOZE

THE STOCKS, HAVERING-ATTE-BOWER

Cranham Honey Cake

Large quantities of honey are made in Essex, of which this cake takes full advantage.

½ lb. self-raising flour	Grated lemon rind
2 eggs	2 oz. glacé cherries,
5 oz. margarine	chopped
2½ oz. caster sugar	Pinch of salt
3 oz. thick honey	4 tablespoons milk

Set oven to 375°F or Mark 5. Cream together in a bowl the margarine, sugar and honey. Beat the eggs and then beat them into the mixture. Fold in the sieved flour, salt, cherries and lemon rind. Add the milk and mix well. Turn into a greased and floured 7-inch round cake tin. Bake for one hour until golden brown. Allow to cool in the tin before turning out.

Southend Fruit Shells

A sponge and fruit berries delight made as individual puddings, originally in scallop shells.

4 oz. butter	1 fl. oz. milk
4 oz. caster sugar	3 oz. raspberries
2 eggs	3 oz. blackcurrants
6 oz. plain flour	Juice of 1 lemon
1 teaspoon baking powder	1 tablespoon sugar
Few drops vanilla essence	Fruit leaves
Scallop shells or pyrex shell-shaped dishes.	

Set oven to 350°F or Mark 4. In a bowl, cream together the butter and sugar. Beat the eggs well and gradually add to the creamed mixture. Sift the flour and baking powder together and fold into the mixture. Add the vanilla essence and enough milk to form a soft, dropping consistency. Grease the shells and divide the sponge mixture between them. Cook for 15 minutes or until well risen and golden brown. Meanwhile stew the fruit with the sugar and lemon juice. Allow to cool. When the sponge shells have cooled, slice into the sponge lengthways, but not all the way through, and fill with the stewed fruit. Decorate with fruit leaves. Makes about 6–8 shells.

PRIORS NEAR BROOMFIELD

Essex Shortcakes

*These biscuits are made to a shortcake recipe with currants added
and sprinkled with sugar before baking.*

9 oz. self raising flour	1 oz. lard
2 oz. sugar	1½ oz. currants
3 oz. margarine	1 fl oz. milk
Sugar for sprinkling	

Set oven to 400°F or Mark 6. Sift the flour into bowl and add the
sugar. Rub in the fats, then add the currants. Gradually mix in the
milk until the mixture binds together. Gently roll out the mixture
to ½-inch thick on a lightly floured surface and then cut into slices.
Place on a greased baking tray and sprinkle sugar over the top of
the biscuits. Bake for about 10 minutes until pale golden brown.
Remove the biscuits from the baking sheet while still warm and
transfer to a wire rack to cool. Makes about 12-16 slices.

Colne Chicken

A grilled chicken dish from the Colne Valley.

4 chicken breasts, boned and
  skinned
8 rashers of streaky bacon
Juice of one lemon

½ tablespoon chopped sage
1 tablespoon chopped parsley
1 tablespoon of chopped
  thyme

Grated rind of one lemon

Set the grill to hot. Flatten the chicken breasts with a wet knife and
cut in half lengthways. Brush the chicken pieces with lemon juice.
Mix together all the herbs and sprinkle each piece of chicken with
the herbs and lemon rind. Wrap a rasher of streaky bacon around
each piece of chicken and grill until cooked. Serve two pieces of
chicken to each person with roast or sauté potatoes and a green
vegetable. Serves 4.

ALRESFORD MILL NEAR WIVENHOE

COCKLES – LEIGH CREEK

Essex Cockle Soup

Leigh-on-Sea is the centre of the Essex cockle industry, where thousands of the shell fish are boiled daily in the cocklesheds.

4 slices smoked streaky bacon, chopped	1 large glass dry white wine
	Water
4 tomatoes	Black pepper
4 medium new potatoes	Tablespoon chopped parsley
2 onions, peeled and chopped	2 pints of cockles in their shells

Fry the bacon until crisp then set aside. Peel the tomatoes by placing them in hot water for 5 minutes, then chop roughly. Peel and dice the potatoes. Fry the potatoes, onions and tomatoes in the bacon fat. When the onions are transparent add the wine, bring to the boil and transfer to a large saucepan. Add sufficient water to cover the mixture, season with pepper and simmer until the potatoes are tender. Meanwhile, clean the cockles throughly, place in a saucepan with a little water, cover and cook until they open. Remove the cockles from their shells and put together with their cooking liquor into the soup pan. Serve at once, topped with the bacon and the chopped parsley. Serves 4.

Chelmsford Pudding

A baked desert made with stewed fruit according to the season.

2 oz. butter	4 oz. self raising flour
2 oz. sugar	Pinch of salt
1 egg	6 oz. stewed fruit, as
¼ pint milk	available in season
Sugar for sprinkling	

Set oven to 350°F or Mark 4. In a bowl, beat the butter and sugar to a cream. In another bowl, beat the egg and add the milk to it. Add the flour and milk/egg mixture alternately to the butter/sugar mixture. Beat well. Add salt. Arrange the stewed fruit in a greased 2 pint pie dish and pour the sponge mixture over. Bake for 30–40 minutes. Remove from the oven and sprinkle the top with sugar. Serve hot with custard. Serves 4.

Essex Pumpkin Pie

An Autumn pudding containing pumpkin, apple and dried fruit.

1 lb. ripe pumpkin, diced	1 teaspoon mixed spice
½ lb. apple, diced	1 teaspoon ground ginger
½ lb. currants	Juice of a lemon
½ lb. sultanas	¾ lb. shortcrust pastry
4 oz. brown sugar	Egg white for brushing

Sugar for sprinkling

Set oven to 400°F or Mark 6. Mix together in a bowl all the ingredients and put the mixture into a large pie dish; oval or round about 9 inches in diameter and 1½–2 inches deep. Roll out the pastry on a lightly floured surface and cover the pumpkin mixture. Brush with egg white and sprinkle with sugar. Put in the oven and bake for 20 minutes. Then reduce the temperature to 350°F or Mark 4 and bake for a further 20 minutes, or until the pastry is golden brown. Serves 6.

Saffron Cake

The purple-petalled autumn flowering crocus which gave the town of Saffron Walden the first part of its name was widely cultivated in the locality until the end of the 18th century for culinary and cloth-dying purposes. The yellow saffron is obtained from the crocus stamens.

12 oz. self raising flour	¼ pint milk
8 oz. currants	4 oz. sultanas
4 oz. butter	2 oz. candied peel
2 eggs	3 oz. brown sugar

¼ teaspoon saffron

Set oven to 350°F or Mark 4. Put the saffron into the milk in a bowl to extract the flavour and stand in the oven for 30 minutes; remove from oven and set aside to cool. Meanwhile, cream together in a bowl the butter and sugar, mix in the flour and then the currants and sultanas. Beat in the eggs and the saffron milk. Mix well and put the mixture into a greased 9-inch round cake tin and bake in the oven for 1½ hours until golden brown.

AT ONGAR

Asparagus Pudding

This 19th century Essex recipe makes a delicate first course.

2 dessertspoons minced ham	A knob of butter
4 eggs, beaten	½ lb. asparagus
1 dessertspoon flour	A few tarragon leaves,
Salt and pepper	chopped

Mince the ham finely and in a bowl, combine with the well-beaten eggs, flour, salt and pepper and the butter. Cut the top part of the asparagus spears into very small pieces and, together with the chopped tarragon, mix with the other ingredients. Then add enough milk to produce a thick, creamy consistency. Pour into a well-buttered mould or pudding basin, cover in foil and steam for 2 hours. Turn out on to a warmed serving dish and pour melted butter round the pudding. Serve hot with hot buttered toast. Serves 4.

NEAR BADDOW RODNEY

Cressing Biscuits

Plain biscuits filled with a butter cream from Cressing near Braintree.

4 oz. plain flour	½ teaspoon bacarbonate
3 oz. sugar	of soda
2 oz. margarine	1 teaspoon baking powder
2 oz. lard	1 teaspoon hot water
1 cup rolled oats	1 teaspoon golden syrup

BUTTER CREAM

5 oz. icing sugar, 3 oz. margarine: Vanilla essence

Set oven to 350°F or Mark 4. In a bowl cream together the margarine, lard and sugar. Sift the flour together with the bicarbonate of soda and the baking powder and mix into the creamed mixture, together with the oats, syrup and hot water. Form into 24 walnut size balls and cook, well spaced, on a greased baking sheet for 10–15 minutes. Transfer to a wire rack to cool. Make up the butter cream by beating together the icing sugar, margarine and a little vanilla essence and use to sandwich the biscuits when cold.

Stuffed Lettuce Hearts

An old recipe for lettuce leaves filled with a pork, egg and herb stuffing.

6 oz. cooked pork, skinned and cubed	2 oz. softened butter
2 hardboiled eggs, peeled and finely chopped	1 tablespoon chopped parsley and chives mixed
¼ teaspoon ground mace	8 crisp heart-leaves of lettuce
½ teaspoon salt	½ cucumber, peeled and
¼ teaspoon pepper	finely sliced

2 oz. finely chopped walnuts

Mix together the pork, eggs, mace, salt and pepper and stir into the softened butter in a bowl. Add the chopped parsley and chives and mix well. Arrange the cucumber slices on four small plates. Divide the stuffing into 8 equal amounts and fill each lettuce leaf with a portion of the stuffing. Put 2 leaves on each plate with the cucumber. Sprinkle with walnuts and chill in the refrigerator for not more than 2 hours. Serves 4.

EAST GATE, COLCHESTER

Pigeon and Parsnip Casserole

Keeping down the pigeon population is a continual battle for countrymen.
Here pigeons are converted into a tasty casserole with parsnips.

4 pigeons, plucked and dressed	2 onions, chopped
2 small parsnips	2 oz. butter
4 oz. unsmoked streaky bacon, chopped	1 dessertspoon flour
	Salt and pepper
	Bunch of herbs

Blanch the parsnips in boiling salted water for a few minutes. Drain, cut into slices and set aside and keep the water. In a pan, sauté the pigeons in the butter until brown on all sides. Add the chopped bacon and chopped onions. Then sprinkle with flour. Mix well and add the parsnip cooking water and the sliced parsnips. Season, add the herbs and cook over a low heat until tender. Serve with creamed potatoes and a green vegetable. Serves 4.

Colchester Pudding

A pudding containing tapioca and stewed fruit topped with meringue.

$1\frac{3}{4}$ pints milk
$1\frac{1}{2}$ oz. tapioca
Pinch of salt
Grated lemon rind
Vanilla essence

1 lb. stewed fruit, as
   available in season
6 egg yolks
$\frac{1}{2}$ lb. caster sugar
5 fl oz. double cream

3 egg whites

Heat oven to 400°F or Mark 6. Heat 1 pint of the milk in a pan, sprinkle on the tapioca with a pinch of salt and bring to the boil. Simmer over a gentle heat until soft. After 10 minutes add the lemon rind and a few drops of vanilla essence. Put a layer of stewed fruit in the bottom of an ovenproof dish and cover with the tapioca. Make a rich custard from the remaining milk, the egg yolks and 3 oz. of the sugar. Heat the milk slowly in a saucepan until just simmering; remove from the heat. Meanwhile mix together the egg whites and sugar in a large bowl. Gradually whisk the cooled milk into the egg mixture, pour back into the saucepan over a gentle heat, whisking all the time until it thickens. Then stir in the cream and pour the custard over the tapioca. Next whisk the egg whites until stiff and spoon in the remaining sugar. Pipe this meringue mixture over the custard. Put in the oven and bake until the top is brown. Serves 4–6.

THE COLNE ESTUARY

Essex Apple Slices

A sponge caked topped with lemon icing and cut into slices.

1 medium cooking apple
Juice of ½ lemon
½ lb. self raising flour
¼ teaspoon baking powder
Pinch of salt

4 oz. margarine
4 oz. caster sugar
¼ pint milk
1 egg
Little melted fat

ICING

½ lb. sifted icing sugar, 3 teaspoons lemon juice

Set oven to 375°F or Mark 5. Peel, core and chop the apple finely and mix with the lemon juice. Sift the flour, salt and baking powder into a bowl and rub in the margarine. Beat the milk and egg together and stir thoroughly into the mixture together with the chopped apple. Brush an 11-inch x 7-inch shallow baking tin with melted fat. Pour the mixture into the tin and spread evenly. Bake for 45 minutes. Make the icing by mixing the icing sugar with the lemon juice and just enough water to make a thick spreading consistency. Pour the icing on to the top of the cake whilst still warm and spread evenly. Allow to cool in the tin and when cold cut into 16 slices.

Stuffed Whole Plaice

In this recipe the whole fish is filled with a cheese and mushroom stuffing.

4 small plaice
(about 12oz. each)
4 oz. Cheddar cheese
2 oz. white breadcrumbs

1 teaspoon dry mustard
2 teaspoons parsley
Juice of ½ a lemon
1 egg, beaten

Set oven to 375°F or Mark 5. Make a cut lengthwise down the centre of each fish and loosen the flesh on both sides of the cut to form a pocket. To make the stuffing, grate the cheese and mix with the breadcrumbs, mustard, parsley, lemon juice and beaten egg. Spoon the stuffing into the pocket of each fish. Place the fish in a buttered baking dish, dot with butter and cover with kitchen foil. Bake for 20–30 minutes. Serves 4.

THE NAZE TOWARDS HARWICH

Kitchels

*It was the custom for the newly-elected Mayor of Harwich to throw kitchels
from the window of the Guildhall to the children
in the street below.*

1 lb. puff pastry	2 oz. ground almonds
2 oz. butter	½ teaspoon ground cinnamon
8 oz. currants	½ teaspoon ground nutmeg
3 oz. chopped mixed peel	Sugar for sprinkling

Set oven to 425°F or Mark 7. Divide the pastry in half and roll each
piece into a thin square on a lightly floured surface. Melt the butter in a saucepan and mix in the currants, peel, almonds and spices.
Spread this filling mixture evenly on one of the pastry squares to
within ½-inch of the edges, moisten the edges with water and cover
with the second piece of pastry. Press together and seal the edges.
Mark the top into 2 inch squares without cutting through. Bake for
25 minutes until well risen and golden brown. Sprinkle with caster
sugar and divide whilst still warm.

AT MESSING

Courting Cake

When an Essex boy was courting an Essex girl, she made this cake for him. If he liked the way it was cooked, he married her!

SPONGE MIXTURE
3 eggs, 3 oz. caster sugar, 3 oz. plain flour, pinch of salt, pinch of baking powder

SWEET SHORTCRUST PASTRY
6 oz. plain flour, 3 oz. margarine, 1 tablespoon sugar, 1 egg

FRUIT FILLING
1 lb. cooking apples peeled and chopped, 1 oz. sugar, 1 tablespoon lemon juice

BUTTER ICING
4 oz. icing sugar, 1 oz. butter

Set oven to 375°F or Mark 5. *Sponge mixture*: whisk the eggs and sugar together in a bowl until thick and creamy. Sift and fold in the flour, salt and baking powder with a metal spoon. *Pastry*: rub the fat into the flour, then add the sugar, bind with the egg and, if needed, a little water. *Fruit filling:* cook the apples with the sugar and lemon juice. Roll out the pastry on a lightly floured surface and use to line a 9-inch deep cake tin. Pour in the apple filling and then pour the sponge mixture on top of the apples. Cook for 25–35 minutes. Allow to cool in the tin. *Butter icing:* beat together the icing sugar and butter until smooth and creamy and use to spread over the cake when cold.

Sautéed Pigeon Breasts

Cooked with celery, this dish is a favourite with rough shooters.

8 pigeon breasts	1 garlic clove, chopped
2 oz. butter	2 sticks celery, chopped
1 large glass of white wine	Salt and pepper
1 onion, peeled and chopped	2 sprigs tarragon

In a pan, sauté the pigeon breasts in the butter until golden brown on all sides. Add the wine, onion, garlic and chopped celery. Season, cover the pan and simmer for 20 minutes. Add the tarragon and continue to simmer, uncovered, for a further 15 minutes. Serve with mashed potatoes and a green vegatable. Serves 4.

Potted Ham

This potted ham, from an 18th century recipe, will keep for two months if the seal is unbroken.

2 tablespoons vegetable oil	$\frac{1}{2}$ oz. curry powder
8 oz. onion, peeled and sliced thinly	1 teaspoon paprika
	Salt
1 lb. cooked ham	$\frac{1}{4}$ pint cider or red wine
$\frac{1}{2}$ teaspoon cayenne pepper	2 oz. butter

Heat the oil in a frying pan and add the onions. Fry until tender, but not browned. Finely mince the ham and onions together. Add the spices and mix well together. Add salt to taste. Put the cider or red wine into a saucepan and add the ham mixture. Mix well, Simmer over a low heat for 30 minutes. Remove from the heat and allow to cool. Pack the mixture into stone, pottery or glass jars. Melt the butter in a saucepan over a low heat. Skim off the foam and strain the yellow liquid into a bowl, leaving the milky residue in the pan. Pour the clarified butter on to the surface of the ham mixture to seal and cover with paper covers. If the butter seal in unbroken the paste will keep for 2 months in the refrigerator.

LUSTY WINTER – STANBRIDGE

Pheasant with D'Arcy Spice Apples

An easy way to cook pheasant casserole. If D'Arcy Spice apples are not available, then Egremont Russet will make a satisfactory alternative.

1 pheasant	4 juniper berries
2¼ lbs. D'Arcy Spice apples	Pinch of thyme
2 oz. butter	1 bayleaf
1 onion, chopped	1 glass of apple juice
Salt and pepper to taste	

Peel and core the apples, leave them whole and set aside. In a pan, sauté the pheasant in the butter until golden brown on all sides. Add the chopped onion, herbs, berries, seasoning and apple juice; surround with the apples and simmer until tender. Serve with the pan juices, thickened with a little cornflour if preferred and with roast potatoes or game chips and a green vegetable. Serves 2.

Roast Pork with Walnut and Spinach Stuffing

Roast spare rib of pork with an unusual and delicious local stuffing.

3 lb. spare rib of pork, boned	3 oz. cooked long grain rice
4 oz. spinach	
1 oz. butter	2 oz. chopped walnuts
1 onion, chopped	1 egg
4 rashers of smoked streaky bacon, chopped	1 tablespoon double cream
	Salt and pepper

Set oven to 350°F or Mark 4. Wash the spinach and remove the stalks. Boil for 2 minutes in very little water, drain well and chop. Set aside and keep hot. Melt the butter in small pan, add the chopped onion and cook for 5 minutes. Add chopped bacon and fry until cooked. Remove from the heat and stir in all the other ingredients and the spinach and season. Mix well and stuff the pocket in the pork left by the removal of the blade bone. Roll up and tie round with string. Roast for 2 hours. Serve sliced with vegetables. Serves 8.

HATFIELD PEVEREL

Devilled Whitebait

Every year a blessing of the first whitebait catch is held at Southend. This fish is caught in large numbers along the South Essex coast.

1 lb. whitebait	½ teaspoon chilli powder
4 tablespoons plain flour	Black pepper
2 teaspoons curry powder	Lemon wedges

Oil for frying

Wash the whitebait, dry well on kitchen paper and set aside. Put the flour with the other dry ingredients in a bowl and mix well. Heat the oil very hot in a deep pan. Coat the whitebait in the seasoned flour and fry in the oil, a few at a time, until crisp (about 2–3 minutes). Remove with a slotted spoon and drain on crumpled kitchen paper. Keep the cooked whitebait hot in the oven until they are all cooked. Serve with thick lemon wedges and buttered brown bread. Serves 4.

Leek Pudding

A traditional boiled suet pudding filled with leeks to accompany boiled or casseroled meats.

6 oz. leeks	3 oz. shredded suet
8 oz. plain flour	4 fl oz. cold water
1 teaspoon baking powder	½ teaspoon salt

Wash and dry the leeks and cut them into thin round slices. Sift together the flour, salt and baking powder into a bowl and add the suet. Mix to a firm dough with cold water. On a lightly floured surface roll out the dough into a rectangle about ¼-inch thick. Spread the leeks liberally over the dough and sprinkle with salt to taste. Roll up from a short end, wrap in a clean pudding cloth and tie each end with string. Place in a saucepan of boiling water and simmer for 1½–2 hours. This pudding is delicious served with Maldon Boiled Beef. Serves 4–6.

Barley Cream Soup

A recipe from the 18th century when Essex was a considerable barley-growing county.

4 oz. pearl barley	¼ pint double cream
1¾ pints chicken stock	Salt and pepper
¼ pint milk	1 oz. butter
2 teaspoons chopped parsley	

Blanch the barley by placing in a bowl and pouring on boiling water: Leave for 1 minute and then drain. Add the drained barley to the chicken stock in a saucepan and simmer for 2 hours. Liquidise the barley mixture and then add to it the milk, cream, salt and pepper, and the butter cut up into small pieces. Return to the saucepan, reheat and then serve sprinkled with the chopped parsley. Serves 6.

METRIC CONVERSIONS

The weights, measurements and oven temperatures used in the preceding recipes can be easily converted to their metric equivalents.

Weights

Avoirdupois	Metric
1 oz.	just under 30 grams
4 oz. (¼ lb.)	app. 115 grams
8 oz. (½ lb.)	app. 230 grams
1 lb.	454 grams

Liquid Measures

Imperial	Metric
1 tablespoon (liquid only)	20 millilitres
1 fl. oz.	app. 30 millilitres
1 gill (¼ pt.)	app. 145 millilitres
½ pt.	app. 285 millilitres
1 pt.	app. 570 millilitres
1 qt.	app. 1.140 litres

Oven Temperatures

	°Fahrenheit	Gas Mark	°Celsius
Slow	300	2	140
	325	3	158
Moderate	350	4	177
	375	5	190
	400	6	204
Hot	425	7	214
	450	8	232
	500	9	260

ST. PETER'S-ON-THE-WALL, BRADWELL